BLOSSOM

The Garden Of Words and Poetry

by

Christine Oberas Aurelio

COPYRIGHT @ 2023 BLOSSOM: The Garden Of Words and Poetry

by Christine Oberas Aurelio

ISBN:

Hardbound-978-621-470-357-9
Softbound/Paperback-978-621-470-358-6
MOBI/KINDLE-978-621-470-359-3

Published by:
Poetry Planet Book Publishing House
Rosario, Pozorrubio, Pangasinan, Philippines
Contact Number: 09554960094
Email: maritesritumalta@gmail.com

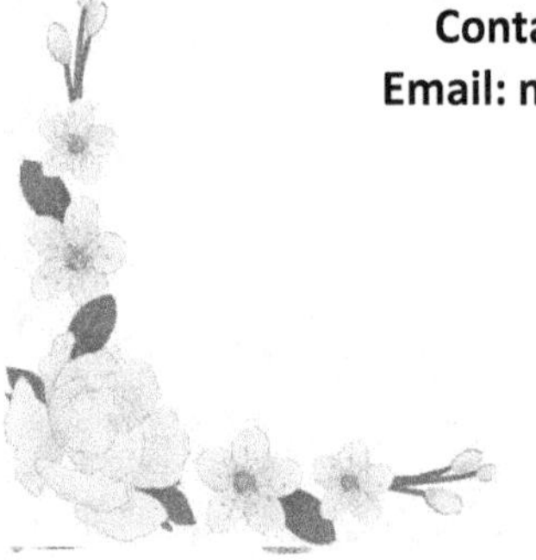

<u>DEDICATION</u>

To my parents for always loving me

To my superheroes

To my prayer warriors

To those who support me

To those who encourage me to bloom

To those who dare to hope

To my wonderful readers

And to the strong person I know: ME.

<u>PREFACE</u>

This book, Blossom is a collection of poems inspired by the author's life experiences, personal growth, struggles, and love while living in a different environment. This serves as an outlet of expression and the best transformational element of being, whereas Poetry seems to be a journey that carries us into valiant adventures. With a melodious pattern of sentences from an intimate creativity of the writer's heart, mind, and soul.

TABLE OF CONTENTS

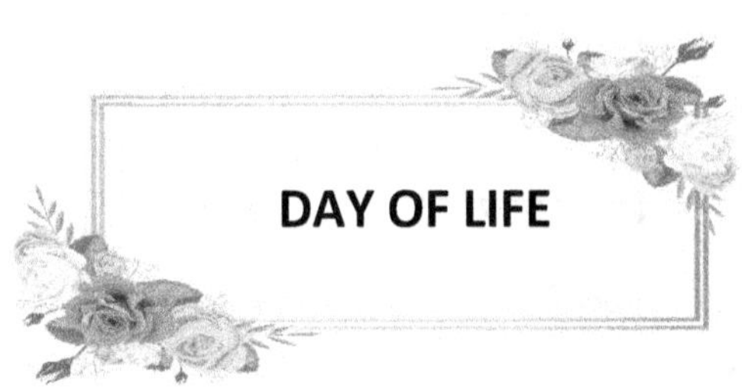

DAY OF LIFE

Look to this day!
Our to-day and yesterday
Cheer up, for the world is young
The best song hasn't been sung
If you can wait and not tired of waiting
Or being hated, don't give way of hating
Life is real! Life is earnest!
Dust Thou art, to dust returnest
But thy eternal summer shall not fade
Nor shall Death brag thou wander'st in his shade,

Sources
Salutation Of The Dawn / Kalidasa
Opportunity / Berton Braley
The Builders / Henry Wadsworth Longfellow
If / Rudyard Kipling
Psalm Of Life / Henry Wadsworth Longfellow
Sonnet 18 / William Shakespeare

Cento Poetry Form

POWERFUL FLOWER

Life start as a small bud under the sun
In the grassland of beauty and romance
Thunder and lightning never let me down
Powerful flower in elegant dance
Rainstorm splashes in my tiny petals
A floating pastel fearless in the dark
Blooming with everlasting scent of love
Powerful flower of peace to remark
In wilderness, I'm standing without doubts
Unspoken words to express from the past
Sweet memories in different shadow
Powerful flower, the fragrance that blast
As the night comes in different glitters
Listening to the music in the breeze
Waiting for the fresh dew to drops and taste
Powerful flower with positive keys

RED STORMY DAYS

Desert country intensely hot
Every house there is a teapot
Roasted chicken and red rice
With exotic aroma of allspice
Red stormy place
Where I heard music of disgrace
Lion and tiger roar so freak
Three little mice creak
Red stormy weather
Work hard to wear a leather
Reflection of agony and fears
Why I am here? Wasting tears
Red color of the day come to end
Dust and stormy journey bend
Now I see the color of life
Hope and courage in nightlife
I won't belong in broken gears
Not in a place where my skin sears
I'll be to wilderness and peaks
Florets, summer breeze and creeks
In every blade of grass
And rustling leaves amass
Where love and respect consist
Love never fade and exist

SWEET MISERY

I saw glitters in the dark light
A joyful noise to hear it right
Loud whisper in my ears that hold
Open secret to keep it cold
Sweet misery wink in my mind
A firm pillow is hard to find
I'm wishing for endless hour to have
It loosely sealed and mess in halve
Small crowd of words to say it wise
It drag me upward fall to arise
Terrible beauty of my unique life
Original copy with different strife

Oxymoron

YESTERDAY'S NIGHTMARE

From the messy busy street
A horrible noise excrete
Surrounded of creepy wall
And in disguise the clumsy bridge fall
The tip toe is in nowhere
Looking for a homely care
Nonsense words was screaming
Unhappy eyes without gleaming
In a cosy bed
With pillow for tears to shed
Crazy place and smelly loom
There is a dark mirror in the room
The yesterday's nightmare
Was a terrifying course to share
And the sketchy scar
A dying reflection from afar

Cacophony

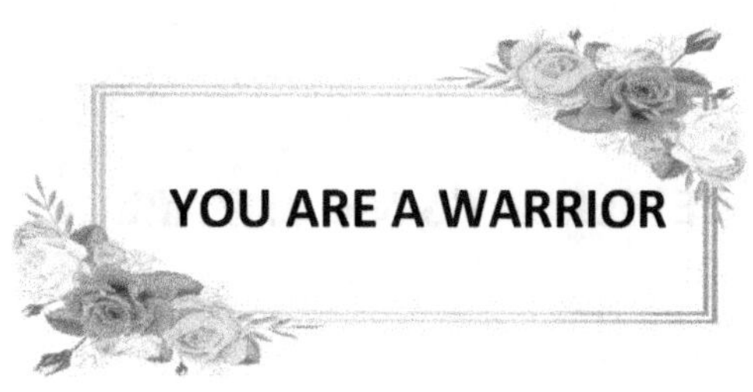

YOU ARE A WARRIOR

When it start to rain and hail
Be a fearless snail
When the sky turns dark
Just remember the sun will rise again and spark
Don't let the beetles get you down
Buckle up and face the hurdles around
Life is just a name
Don't quit, just prepare for a game
Being fast is not enough to run the race
Take it easy and feel the steps with a loving grace
Keep going, never lose your fight
Breathe and scroll for everything shall be all right
So it is time to leave your failures behind
And forget the word "stop" in your mind
Birds and a rainbow asking for you to go along
Storms are made for you to be strong
No matter how hard it is, you are going to make it
You are a warrior, and you need to admit
Try and you will get there in the end
Just do your best to find a way.

VOICELESS STRANGER

We fly and sail a thousand miles away from home
Poverty pushed us to leave our place before gloom
Years of emptiness is what we feel and speak
A hundred of opportunity is what we seek
Torn between feelings of being separated and
sadness
Mistreatment and racism against us in badness
We're carrying the citizenship without rights
Discrimination sucks our bone but everyday we
must fight
Our ears were blocked from the pesky voice
Listening to some insult is one of the choice
We are cretin is what they say
Even our leg are popping from long hours working
with no delay
Anxiety grows because of an abusive hand
Respect that we ask is hard for them to understand
We are craving for a plate of food
But then, we're very grateful for leftovers to
express our gratitude
Every month we're waiting for our sacrifice to be
paid
In a big dismay salary was cut and cheated

The colored and long agreement was neglected
No one heard our humble quench as always it was
rejected
Stories of grief and tears is what we hide
Voiceless stranger in purpose is to provide
Why we've been accused?
We just aim for love not a single bruise
A new home and new identities in the unknown
In a blind society we're breaking stereotypes alone
Words to speak in silence, yes We know that we
don't belong
Our loved ones ask, why we take so long?

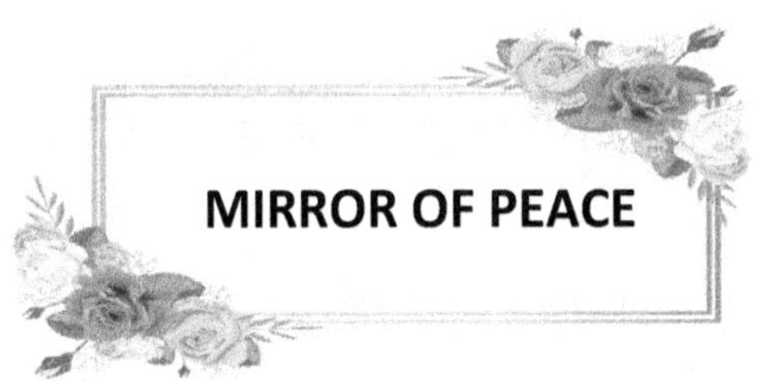

MIRROR OF PEACE

As the tree reaching its arms to the sky
The wind stays above so the leaves can fly
Clear water the mirror of peace
Our world is full of wonderful pieces
The nature tell me of who I am
It reminds me that I am sweet as a yam
I heard nameless sound in several faces
Why I'm chasing answer for some cases
Seeing the motionless reflection of a lake
My soul was amazed and awake
I want to touch the sleeping element
To change the tune of my old instrument
My desire to cross and wash away my fears
In the verdure color without shadow of tears.

IRREPLACEABLE

Shadow behind a ray of light
In this treacherous life we flight
Even in rainy days and feeling blue
Something irreplaceable and true
A bond full of memories in the dark
But like moon and stars that spark
We treasure it as a gold
Hands of comfort to hold
Beauty with a pure heart
Sweet word with trust to start
From a garden of tears and pain
To the flowers that bloom in plain
Shining tincture that's so special to me
Vivid colors with purpose to see
A shoulder to lean on to balance a boat
To protect me from sinking and float
My strong support when I have to try
In happiness and sorrow when I cry
It doesn't require effort and time
Things to remain so prime
The chapter to keep writing new pages each day
To walk and guide in our way
The meaning of selfless love.
Destiny and blessings from above

THE MUSE

I am the muse and inspiration
A fruit bearing tree of the nation
With dignity to lead and rise
Giving a new life in different ties
My roots are the beginning of history
Digging and crawling to unanswered mystery
Heavy rain dripping on my steam
Little twigs and blossom in a dream
Swaying in the midst of storm
Waiting for the sun for me to reform
Strong branches carrying my leaves
I'm weak is what they believes
To share the sweetness of my crop
The tiny seed breathe in every drop
Patience show in the cooling shade
A love to give for a decade
I am the melody of Silent River
The best rhymes across the land to deliver
I am the echo that you always hear
Don't let my own figure disappear.

GLOOMY EYESHOT

In unknown road full of query
A shadow ahead in shrubs pieri
Gloomy eyeshot insight to form a knot
Imagination of connecting several dot
Way to follow and wonder
Desire and effort that make us under
Foggy future in our own mind
The answer is not easy to find
Behind the light are doubts
Let fear and negativity out
Be strong to face the reality beyond
Determination is the best bond
Pass the challenge of being alone
In diverse ground, your power to be blown
Believe that there comes a season
Your existence is one of the reason

THE HOMELESS

I am here and there
Everybody sees but no one care
If it is my fate
Why others laugh and hate
I'm in the shadow of nothing
Your kindness is what I'm asking
I wish to live in a closed wall
To hide my pain big and small
The street is widely open but not for me
This kind of journey, I don't want to be
I am useless but full of hope
I'm in agony looking for the right scope
I saw patriarch walking with tigers around
While I'm sleeping with cockroach on the ground
I saw them wearing in a heavy gold
My lips are dry, I'm freezing with cold
In the dark alone
Having no place to call my own
The sound of tiptoes passing by
Raising my hand waiting them to reply
My heart is broken
Hunger is always outspoken
I am homeless, the forgotten part
In the society of being departed.

LITTLE TWIG

From little twig in a tree
Life with variant color as we see
Crackling large holes in the bud
Crystal water that flows from a mud
Day by day it grows
Today and tomorrow that we borrow
Beauty swaying with the wind
Dancing while starving as we bind
Embracing changes of time
Letting go to sublime
Trust the natural process
Better human being to reprocess
Feel the sound of reality
Upgrade ourselves' mentality
Glance at the dazzling background
Leaves flew to the ground.

BLOODED ROPE

War will never be good in speech
Peace seems to beyond our reach
Killing and destruction of property
Suffering humanity, life of poverty
Slow down the progress of mankind
Evil, horror in blooded rope defined
Oh God, please heal our land
Hatred between nations
Dreams, hope devastation
Trauma to children and all civilian
Economy goes down and losses of billion
Education has gone, school was destroyed
Unsafe, violence so annoyed
Soldiers and families separation
Crying in pain, weep of action
Oh God, please heal our land
Let's be kind to one another
Kindness is a way to love others
Stop the war for it is created by man
War is not the solution, its danger for human
Negotiate, listen and understand
Eternal peace is in our hand.

TEMPORARY TIDE

Take your own boat and sail with gloat
Don't ever stop just take a note
Things to rewrite when the wind swap
Do some hop but don't be a flop
We must survive to be alive
Remove all your fears, enjoy the strive
Life that you live with faith in spear
A reason to cheer without tears
Sadness or blue it will get new
Every race will change like dew
Without any clue in God's grace
Game we must face, life to embrace
Perfect as can be, stay to see
Temporary tide in the sea
Discover for free, love is our guide
Do not hide the happiness inside

POEM IS A GARDEN

Poem is a garden of essence
Tend haecceity for convalescence
With fragrant perfume of flowers
Long lasting aroma of woman empowers
Poem is an emblem of diversity
A world of biodiversity
Poem is a quieten ocean of mystery
A heart to know the protohistory
Poem is a galaxy of splendid thoughts
Million of stars to explore as an astronauts
A planet that reflects light
A dozen of moons that shine so bright
Poem is a cosmic snowballs
A frozen fire so magical as it falls
Poem is an earth where we exist
A world of life full of twist
Poem is my exotic beauty
A passion of freedom and equality
Poem is a music, lyric from my heartbeat
You can cry, dance and sing in aesthete
A depiction and connexion of my past
Irrational motive ever last
My power of self-assured with positive mind
A blessings of inspiration for mankind

SHADOW OF THE PAST

Young smile reflection
Fair and lovely complexion
Girl in the mirror with her dreams
Her confidence screams
Who to be in the future?
How to deal with nature?
Beautiful and fresh face
Handsome men will chase
Years pass by
Shadow of past never deny
A face of wrinkles everywhere
And memorable moments to share
Scattered gray hair
An image of respect and care
A senior age in the mirror wall
Words of wisdom to recall
Old portrait from yesterday
Book to take down what they say
Our smile to show
For their kind heart and breath to glow.

LONG BRISTLE

Lying on the ground
When nobody is around
Looking up
Wondering where was my cup
Under the cotton clouds
Why there are no crowds
Lifting my hands to the sky
Wind blows and passes me by
No beeps and whistles
Only the long bristle
Strong branches of the tree
Days and years of being free
From hard walls and chain
The past that I don't want to happen again.

THE BUILDER

Left and right of the road you are standing
Your dedication and hard work is so inspiring
You are the root of a meaningful life
The real hero that sounds in different fife
With dignity from head to hand
Your strength and courage to build our land
Day by day, you're sweating under the sun
To work until night-time is a lot of fun
A single penny is not just what you aim
But to give the best smile in one frame
The respect that you deserve
Beautiful and prosperous nation you serve
From the fields to the deepest sea
Your artwork is so wonderful to see
The pain never let you down
To construct the tallest tower in town
Your kindness to share what you know
Boundless patience is part of the show
Changes in our surroundings appear
The real fighter, truthful and sincere.

INNOCENT EYES

An innocent eyes with a little heart
The image of pure joy and smile from the start
Curiosity that pushes them to know
Tender sweet lips with limited words in a row
Every action is a mystery and magic
For life to them has no tragic
No doubt of what is happening around
Why there is a flying fairy in the ground?
Child face is a wonderful sight
In the dark they glow as a starlight
For another world of fantasy and wonder
Their only fear is to hear the thunder
Let's open our eyes and appreciate things that we
see
Like the tiny souls enjoying their moment for free
Explore the beauty of growing day by day
With mind full of happiness as they play.

LISTEN TO THEM

Blankets and sleeping bags to take
Homes gone was the worst dream to awake
Going here and there to hide with fear
A voice in prayer under the clouds appear
A gray smoke from a burning house
Women in bandage and bloody blouse
An innocent kid running with a toy
Words of sadness, humanity to destroy
The dying dreams of young and old
Kindness to share and peace are gold
Feed our crying sisters and brothers
Love and care to one another
Soldiers risking their own life
To protect family from dangerous strife
Respect and solidarity to the nation
Different story of sorrow and inspiration
Listen to them for they are in pain
A helping hand for their strength to gain
Plead for safety and to end the blooded sword
For justice and people's dignity to stack in cord.

SLOW DOWN

Walking with millions of stars in my head
Some phrases and lines to read
Hurry up! And my steps is getting so fast
Speeding as I can to feel the blast
Numbering my plans to achieve
Everyday I need to be brave
Hoping for the time to agree
I heard a voice inside of me
SLOW DOWN!
Look at the scenery around
Life doesn't have to be a hamster wheel
High speed isn't a deal
Enjoy the present moment
Build and live your life in alignment
Don't forget where you are going
Know your purpose before doing.

APPLE'S EYE

Your smart mouth that kicks me out
Sexy skirt admire you without doubt
The real Romeo from a distance
My moon and only resistance
Anytime I can give you my heart
And every day we can draw a chart
Or together we can ride
And walk with you in the coast and hide
Seeing you is a kind of fragrance
Apple's eye you are the perfect ambiance
A rosy book of you and me
Let's share a cup if you agree
Why you are so gentle like man of cloth
In a burning fire, I'm just a moth
With a sweet throat and delight
Yes I'm dreaming under the basking light.

Metonymy

RISING PATH

A rising path of the unknown
Patience to move in your own
The vision of moving up as a seer
In the horizon, success is what we hear
Every line is a change
Hope and faith arrange
Calmness of the heart
Appreciate your steps to start
Silence that aim to teach
Full determination to reach
Be fearless to pursuit
Your dream is a flute
Don't just stare and think
Keep going, be strong not to sink
Hard work will take you to the top
Enjoy the life journey, do not stop.

BE YOU

Write to remember your hardships and cite
Cite your story, inspiration to write
Make it so beautiful blue like a lake
Lake that calm, clear water silently make
Grow happy to face the wind and breath slow
Slow down in rocky road for you to grow
Today, you start to understand the way
Way to reach the highest peak of today
Share your heart and soul but learn how to care
Care for life, awesome and perfect to share
Feel the light in the dark, now time to seal
Seal without fear, the peace is what you feel
Cry out when you are sad, new game to try
Try to do your best, never doubt and cry
Hope to keep so you can pass the long rope
Rope full of struggle, pull it with your hope
See what you really is in life to be
Be who you are is what I want to see

Mirror Sestet Poetry Form

TIMELESS SOUL

An endless trial and troubles to tell
Sound of doubts echoes inside of me
Should I listen or not?
If I heard that happiness comes in
Dazzling of flowing sand so mournful
New day, new challenges to number
In the complications of life
No matter what shade and color it is
Some days I've lost but
Some are my best win
Extremely strong wind to empty
Fearless to pursuit my dreams
It's all in my mind for
Me to stay to feel the
Shining star of timeless soul
To see what really is
It hits me hard and dead
I know that
God is with me He never slumbers
Something happens and
You will get all the new things
What hold you back is never what you are
But the thought of what you are not
Dark gray behind you then so what?

Just take moment as they
Come savor life whenever you may seem

"A Psalm of Life"
BY HENRY WADSWORTH LONGFELLOW
Tell me not, in mournful numbers,
Life is but an empty dream!
For the soul is dead that slumbers,
And things are not what they seem.

Golden Shovel Poetry Form

THOUSAND DREAM

I feel fresh gale

Real peace to gain

Beat of horse gait

Shiny wood grain

Brown leaves that falls

And river flows

Sweet fruits for food

Frigid ice floes

Sky is so deep

Long legs of deer

A thousand dream

Art life my dear

The time is short

To get a spot

Under the sun

Try your best shot

Train Rannaigechta Moire Poetry

BUCKLE UP

You think you have messed up?
Yup
No, you were not the one behind the case
Base
See what good you have learn
Earn
Buckle up, stand and see
Free
Don't say you are weak
Freak
Just look inside and light up a spark
Dark
Breathe the fresh air out your mind at ease
Please
Pick the sadness in the floor
Door
Life taught us to fight
Right
Life will never be the same
Blame
You will have to go that extra mile
Smile
Situation will throw you out of gear
Dear
Every hour and time extent
Spent

Echo Verse Poetry

THE INNER ME

As I close my eyes
Dark clouds arise
Thunder start roaring
Emotion spark and soaring
Lot of query in my head
The Inner me unsaid
Silence is my voice
The best and golden choice
Memories from the past
A dream that never last
Gushing words of really I am
An old me in whispering bam
It wasn't me
This is not what I want to be
Image of sadness in grey
Realness I've wish to display
Hoping for acceptance around
Being me to be found
Happiness to show to everyone
Pure and real to anyone
Without truth to hide
Telling what and who I am inside
Free from others belief
In most inspirational motif

Change to do what I love
Like a self- governing dove
Creating my own version
I and me conversion
A warrior and fighter
That believe in herself tighter

ARID LAND

Once I was far away
Seeing no tress that sway
Empty piece of ground
Whooshing dry air around
A dazzling arid land
The beauty of reddish yellow sand
Space of silence is what I feel
Flashing of water is a way to heal
Hot and cold weather extreme
Walking it there is kind of redeem
I'm wishing to be a cactus plant
To enjoy the game with an ant
My emotions so high
Rough life I can't deny
Laughing is better for crying
Sand dune climb to keep trying

LET IT GO

The sky was never ending and vast
It was full of mystery that never last
From the little light that spark
With countless diamond in the dark
A peaceful place for the birds to fly
For an eye to see that we must retry
Just outstretch your hand
In blue or grey the moon can stand
I wonder how it ignores
Some laughter, crying and roars
How it was still glowing after the storm
Its own beauty that no one can deform
Let it shine for this is the time
To let go and be one of the prime
It's time to celebrate all your pains
Like a fearless star in the end of rain
With all your effort to grow
In deep silent breeze it really shows
It will be strange
But darkness is our way to change

TWIST AND TURN

From the roaring of waves of the sea
The scent of dirty mud on my knee
Heavy rain that touches my skin
Sharp oyster shell cuts my feet like a pin
Looking up with a prayer on my mind
Please stop the smouldering wind
The slow motion of the boat
Hope is my perfect coat
Seasons come and go
Moving my paddle high and low
As the sun rises from the east
To reach the shore is a feast
My thought of life is not always the same
I must learn the term of the game
When the dawn is dark, I wait for sunlight
To make my world so happy and bright
Poverty that causes me so much pain
Strength for tomorrow to gain
I believe that I can cross the fence
Positivity shall be in every tense
Under the deep blue water
Walking in arid land like a porter
Unexpected twist and turn
Discouragement, doubt and fear to burn.

SWEET ADIEU

I love how the light seeps in through
Mornings is much better with you
The sunray kisses, bright and new
Blossom of heart for us to glue
Just want to send you hugs too
Me and you, a life to renew
Your sweet smile has different hue
To think back the first drop of dew
Unspoken things to say and do
Hold my hand, it's time to be true
In my mind you're the best tattoo
With forever bond to pursue
Moment to treasure in revue
A cosy breakfast food for two
The eternal flame without due
Promises of your sweet adieu.

Monorhyme Poetry

MY SWEET PERFUME

Smile in her face, as time cuts by
Her mighty old trunk was awry
Her strong thorns is getting so weak
Water drops and start to leak
It's not pleasant and it has no grace
I smell the reality she have to face
The emotions that I can't hide
I lost my sweet brier in my side
I will miss her essence
Forever evanescence
Vermillion red cheeks turns to grey
I don't have words to express that day
You're my perfect rose in my heart grows
My sweet perfume in the wind that flows
Your love and struggle is my life
Your tangled roots keep me alive
My one and lovely shrub in my garden
You at peace in the Garden of Eden
Losing your fragrant is not the ending
Leaving me is my new beginning.

FLUTTERING DREAMS

When I was wrapped by darkness
Enfold of pain and sadness
I don't know how to survive
My journey that needs to revive
Fluttering dreams help me to hope
Power and strength for life to cope
Dreaming of floating in the sky
Happiness that I can't deny
Looking for a mesmerizing place to reside
Or perhaps I would live in the hillside
Playing with those fluffy cloud
Shimmering colors I see in crowd
Reflection of rainbow, flowers bloom
Greenery spread, feel no gloom
Why shy away from those stormy nights?
Time to flit too see the lights
I fleet to face the hurdle of the wind
Tent flap to leave my shadow behind
Courage echoes for survival of change
I embrace the process to arrange
Struggle is my strength for today
Obstacles are my stepping way
Every dark cloud is a silver lining
Fly away, taste the flowers that's shining,

GO FISHING

Go fishing and sing
As you see the waves doesn't ring
Oceanic quiet as the tree
And the calm weather agrees
In an aquatic deep blue sea
Swim bladder creature plays with glee
With different attractive colors
Take with you the hook of multicolour
Now time to work your fishing pole
While the wind is under control
Take your time be patience and enjoy
Catching big or small fish it gives life
No matter how old you are
You can be a superstar
Learn the best fishing times
Fishing is a lifetime.

A WAY BEYOND

I found myself alone
In far away, I called my own
Creative vision of life
Steps of hope and strife
My little adventure
Power of dreams full of venture
A way beyond where pretty thoughts
Positivity and confidence in spots
Courage to go afar
Walk on to see how it really are
To keep pushing myself
Sweat and tears itself
A long hours of hard work
Patience for rework
Never give up for this is a chance
Packing my goals to advance
From the ground to the end
Toes of faith to bend
The side of undiscovered
Inspiration of success to recovered.

LIGHT OF ETERNITY

Under the clouds there is a sound
An agony in the ground
Pain and flowing tears
Humble eyes that no one cares
Day to end and start
Sorrow is a part
Run to see the shining lane
Peace is what we seek and gain
Forgiveness to take
Our faith must awake
A path of light till eternity
Clear blue sky of mystery and clarity
Buzzing trumpet while angels sing
Waiting in the gate in white feather wing
Beautiful place to live together
New yet unknown but free
A paradise for you and me

SHE IS LEGENDARY

She is my sunshine on a misty day
She smiles to take my fears away
She always by my side
Memories to share in a single slide
She is the flowers
The sweet kiss and hugs she showers
A thousand splendid scenes and lessons to still
Millions of words to tell
Her greatest strength that inspire me
Her sacrifice and wisdom to see
Her generosity that I salute
My special treasure in a distinct suit
She stood by me
And show me the swath that I can see
Her kindness and patience
Her presence has a beautiful existence
She is special and pure
The brightest star for sure
Her support is my reason to stay
In lost paradise and she raised me up to sway
I respect her with all of my heart
For sharing her life from the start
She in incredible and amazing
She is legendary and forever dazzling.

Sibilance

I WISH

As I look at the sky
How I wish that there'll be no goodbyes
There's no distance and race in every mile
No crying, just a perfect and everlasting smiles
As I hear the wind blow
I'm wishing for healthy seeds to grow
No hungry mouth and empty plates
No more violence and no more hates
How I wish to be a guitar
To strengthen the arms of those from afar
A soul that heals from the melody of my own
The perfect elements to soften the heart of stone
I wish to share a million colors of sound
No one is broken because love is around
How I wish to live in a castle with him
To hold and kiss is what I whim
What if everything in life is all for free
Like picking some leaves falling from the tree
There'll be no poor and rich
I'm wishing there'll be someone to fix the stitch.

GOOD HEART
AND KINDNESS

We are in the beginning to change the world
Under the deep blue skies full of power
You don't have to be great to show respect
Good heart and kindness can calm the glower
Crying in vain, dripping of tears around
Humanity and freedom to collect
Good heart and kindness can calm the glower
You don't have to be great to show respect
Just open your heart to all with a smile
Understand each other and empower
You don't have to be great to show respect
Good heart and kindness can calm the glower
Poverty that pull us down and dying
Be kind for unity to reconnect
Good heart and kindness can calm the glower
You don't have to be great to show respect
The one quality that will stay with you
Love to spread like a colorful flower
You don't have to be great to show respect
Good heart and kindness can calm the glower

Mirror Refrain Poetry

TO MY MOTHER

A dependable source of comfort
You are the kindest soul I know
Guidance that takes me long way
The real wonder woman
My peace in my heart
Standing with me
My mother
I love
You

HERO

Father
First man I ever loved
Hero and beloved
Cheer me on my game
Through the hall of fame
Best friend
You are like that spark
That glows in the dark
Your wisdom and grace
There's peace on your face

COLORS OF LIFE

Colors of life, the tree that gently sway
The hilly air, flowers bloom, smell of rain
Like sky descends, drops pouring, peace to gain
Nature's beauty, wonderful role to play
Silent proof, green fields, quiet night remain
Colors of life, the tree that gently sway
The hilly air, flowers bloom, smell of rain
Enchanting tide, as you look at the bay
Moon so bright, relax and forget the pain
Dew of leaf, day started, sorrows to drain
Colors of life, the tree that gently sway
The hilly air, flowers bloom, smell of rain
Like sky descends, drops pouring, peace to gain.

Madrigal Poetry

A DECADE

My veins are getting stronger each day
Hues of tomorrow to see halfway
A world to set up and renew
As I saw the land in morning dew
Patience that I've been for a decade
The reasons of the worst nightmares and dismayed
Every day of trying to forget the past
Is the most painful things that never last
Those promises from yesterday was gone
Standing alone, wondering what's going on
Beautiful scene that welcomes me in distance
Years in a glimpse of being persistence
Me and my bucket of plans in my head
It's not easy to understand if you don't read

THE GARDENERS

From the most loving hand of our saviour
We grow under the pattern of behavior
Circumstances that we in encounter in life
Human nature in different kind of strife
Light of goodness in our heart
Some changes in societies and art
Golden history has been forgotten
The gardeners to take care of rotten
Pieces of rules that are out of control
Knowledge to reveal the goal
Magnificent thinking to collect
Obstacles to face and reconnect
Understanding of whom we become
Relationship with nature in silent drum
Mankind is the main essence of survival
Existence have choices of revival

LEARN TO TRY

Go to sleep
Dream of life
Days you lose
Without rife
Think about
Write and read
To bring out
Love that spread
Filled with hopes
Broken dreams
Do not waste
Outcast themes
Grow happy
Don't be shy
Beat your fear
You can try

Cethramtu Rannaigechta Moire Poetry

WARM WORDS

Whispering wind whistle
Weak woman wave
Why walking wary
With wing wild weed
War was won
Warm words within
Weapon with wisdom
We write without worry
Wound was wash
White wagon wealth
Warrior willpower
Whimsical worship
Wonderful welcome
Where wish waiting
Worthy wright
Withstand written

Tautogram Poetry

KNITWORK

Knitting is creative to boost my mood
Sitting with colorful yarn new and old
Getting my sharp pair of scissors to cut
Fitting wool scarf and hat perfect for cold
Brain to float and fly to create new style
Gain more patience and practice is the key
Pain of fingers, just relax and have fun
Again , loops and knot to connect and see

Lento Poetry

HEAVEN'S REFLECTION

I wake up to start a new day
To spend my time without dismay
In grassland under heat of the sun
Picking flowers is nearly done
As the stormy day that passes by
To find the highest peak defy
The falling rain that drops on me
Another world is what I see
The chirping sound of bird so sweet
Reminds me to forget defeat

Calm river that flow in between
Shining stones with shadow of green
My moods gets bright seeing the tree
Swaying leaves and fresh air agree
With rhythmic sound to the intense
The smell of clay like an incense
Peace in every breath designed
Serene voice of my blowing mind
Looking at the bay and the wave
Vivid ocean and sky to save
Crossroads and long journey of mine
Darkness night the grace of divine
The twinkling stars are my guide

Listening to my song beside
Seeing this is to know my worth
Wonderful creation on earth
Beauty of heaven's reflection
Amazing God my protection

Modern Pastoral Poetry

MY ONE AND ONLY SPARE

You are the right key to the gate
For you to love me that God create
From darkness that bright
You show me the light
My old key leave me broken
Damaged and unspoken
Now with you I am free
OH, do you give yours to me
You unlocked my heart
Perfect from the start
You've let out the chain
In the room of pain
Nothing can tear us apart
Forever you will be my part
Fit and not fake
You save me in shadow of mistake
Solid and authentic
Pure and aesthetic
You're not silver or gold
You open my heart into a new world
I promise for you to take care
My one and only spare
I keep you safe and proud
I love you out loud

AGELESS MARK

Silver moon
Spot the dark
Black and blue
Ageless mark
Rays of hope
Glare the sea
In silent
Shine on me
Peaceful night
Rise and glow
Be so calm
Winds that blow
The whispers
To complete
Gets the dream
No retreat

UNDEFEATED

She holds everything in her hand
She decides with her best strategies and stand
She is undefeated
And she deserves to be treated
She doesn't let the little voices to be unheard
She can rule the world with her unmovable word
She serves with all her heart
Her care is the foremost part
She is the light of every home
She waters us to become healthy as a loam
She taught us what really life is
The best teacher to teach us how to pass the quiz
Though awful days and restless night
She is strong and able to fight
She sings and smile, but sometimes she is crying
She hides her pain without regrets of trying
She struggled for us to wear a pearl
A smart and pretty, like her when she was a girl
She is the most expensive gem to be treasure
Her boundless love is beyond measure

RED FAIRY TALE

From the tallest and green mountain that speak
They're waiting for the clear blue sky to sneak
The breath of fresh air in sense without mistake
Golden victory is very near in the peak
Beautiful women dry up your tears
For tomorrow is the absence of fears
Father be strong to hold good your daughter
Mother tell your son, be safe in water
Soon this dusky surrounding will last for change
Sweet sunflower to ties you all in range
Let the light of glorious hope be in your heart
With love and unshaken faith that never apart
The power is in your hands so stand still
Remember that you're not alone in the hill
Shine for it is yours, the landscape and beauty
To protect your fellowmen is one of your duty
For today is just going to be a red fairy tale
History to write and share with full of detail
Weapon to lay down for humility and wisdom
A sword lily will rise again to stop the storm

THE SEA

The swaying waves and peaceful wind
So sweet horizon in my mind
Of seashore
I breathe deeply to feel the sound
Deep green blue color that surround
In seaside
A healthy source of food under
Savory dish appetizer
From seafood
With colorful pebbles that shine
The elegant beauty in line
Of seashell
Relax under the lovely sky
Release your stress it's free to try
Seawater

Compound Word Verse Poetry

TILL ETERNITY

Come with me my love
Let's fly to heaven above
Hold my hand and say
I want to hear your voice everyday
I carry your heart
And I carry it in my heart
My love for you is glowing
My love for you is growing
Every time I see your face
My heart begins to race
Never forget what you're for me
It will always be you before me
For years I had been looking out
All alone and helpless I shout
I can feel that love along
Let it remain, oh strong
You and I will stay this way
This love will forever stay
Together we dream
We will fight and scream
Our promise to be one
Under the ray of sun
With purity and solidarity
I will love you until eternity

SPIRAL HORIZON

I've been spending time of mounting
Alighting steps and counting
Querying how to climb
Listening to the sound of chime
As I look it seems too high
Heights and number of stairs to defy
A thumping sound in my thorax
My wisdom was pacts
Spiral horizon requiring
Phases of life so inspiring
Path that change the entire me
Quest deep on my knee
Journey of strength and power
Bunch of curiosity to reach the tower
Digging my feet and stand with ease
Confidence for the next chapter to please

BRIGHT NIGHT

Feel alright
The stars are shining so bright
Night gives you a sense to be
See

Think ahead
Plan what you decide instead
Close your eyes and wait for new
Dew

Don't regret
Silence for stress to forget
The peace in your heart is sure
Pure

Deibide Blaise Fri Toin Poetry

MIND POWER

Mind is the human power
Positive thoughts to empower
It speaks what we are from within
Stick on what we believe in
Principles in life ahead
Powerful book to be read
A place where nobody can barge
Beliefs and doubts to recharge
Our secret spot that no one knows
What we blow and grows
It can build and destroy the earth
Lesson to learn how to rebirth
Tool to attain success
Knowledge and positivity confess
It moulds and make a man
Courage in every step of our plan

KIND SOUL

I am a pesky plants that can grow
A fluffy dandelion dancing in glow
Hearty resilient and strong weed
Floating in the wind as a seed
Swaying across the grass land
Wish to touch the ground by hand
So beautiful under the sunlight
Yellow flower blooming bright
Growing up and flying around
Scattered dreams surround
Days of waiting for the season
New phases change without a reason
I'm a golden dandelion and proud
Even no one notice me in the crowd
I can rise and dignify my own
My wings of kind soul to be shown

NEW DAWN

A new dawn brings new light
Be happy with the smile
You have to go that mile
To feel awesome and right
A new dawn brings new light
But you have your own file
May you keep smiling awhile
Morning is really bright
A new dawn brings new light
Get ready for some trail
Message of love to hail
End the darkness and night
A new dawn brings new light

Dansa Poetry

FLOW FREELY

Giving up is not an option to think
Let your eyes never be without a dream
Paddle your own canoe, listen and blink
You flow freely and feel the silent stream
Life is not the same, courage is require
So do not feel sad, you always have chance
Seek the spark, set your vision on fire
Keep that spirit, cherish the waves and dance
Learn how to sing with the whispering wind
Reflect the crystal and shining water
Forget darkness and clear your golden mind
Observe the calming sky like a spotter
Face your sorrows with acceptance and smile
If you thinking you are too small was wrong
Just stay happy to attain extra mile
Have that confidence, focus and be strong

Decasyllabic Poetry

IN MY GIRLHOOD

A thousand of dreams in my girlhood
In the sea house made of wood
Under the clear blue sky
With peaceful wind that lead me to fly
How I wish to bloom like a flower
Grow and sway with its own power
The everlasting scent of life
I know, I need to strive
To create a wonderful song
It gives a radiance and peace along
An innocent and glowing face
Be strong to win the race
I don't know about tomorrow
Picking some petals without sorrow
Chasing butterfly in the grass
Every day is a new story to pass

CLOSE YOUR EYES

Life is a game
To win is what we aim
Everyone has power and skill
Everyone is in their race to fulfil
Don't lose your smile
Running through the hurdles per mile
Looking with people along with you
Or in the trees behind with different hue
Close your eyes
You need to know that the sun will rise
It will give you all light
Cause you have to shine bright
Balance which everyone hold
Shivering hands to mold
Past to wash away with tears
It's time to come and conquer fears
No matter if you're weak or not
You must learn how to tie a knot
Move forward and stand tall
Never be afraid to fall

LIFE HIKES

Life is the best trail way to hike
Obstacles is not to give up
You choose whatever path you like
Life is the best trail way to hike
Big rocks, bumps in the road and dike
In the unknown, with fearless cup
Life is the best trail way to hike
Obstacles is not to give up

Triolet

TIME TO UNTIE

When the night flows in silence
And cricket voice under
I remember how we try
From the bridge of friendship we're holding tight
I'm thinking of you
I'll choose to stay even it's hard
In just a matter of second
It was the worst nightmare, I ever had
In lakes of sadness and tears
From the disaster that strikes me
On the pages of broken promises
I have to get up and leave
Fears and doubts inside me,
It's time to untie the broken rope
This the last time of seeing you
Because I am done and goodbye to you

BLOW, BLOW

Blow blow, let the wind blow
To the leaf that slowly grow
On a hot and sunny day
Blow blow, let the wind sway
Help birds to fly and sing
Blow blow, let the spring wind swing
Please, I want my wind pin spin
Blow blow, Please touch my skin
Those branches in the breeze
The quiet music of trees
Listen and let your heart feel
Blow blow, let the wind tell

Repetition

I SAW WATER

I saw water stream flows into the sea
And now the swaying grass under the tree
A slender shadow of dazzling sun
Our season change, birds was shot by gun
Why castle was built with different key
The scent of patrons on stage disagree
While the doer sweeps chimney on bending knee
I'm listening stories of hills and fun
I saw water
Like glass walls scout the reflection of me
Shell was wash and furnish for some degree
The show of being a runner begun
I'm playing and catching waves one on one
Over the rough rocks of pain, yes I'm free
I saw water

Rondeau Poem

TOUCH OF SINCERITY

Quality of being human
Society, man and woman
Humanity is caring others
Respect to one another's
Absence of selfishness
Unity means togetherness
Serving the poor
Refugee knocking to our door
Religious rite
We must know our rights
Freedom of speech
Equality to teach
Humanity is to feed
To those who need
The cease of poverty
Not for fame but a touch of sincerity
Open your heart
Is a simple start
Listen to agony
Love to live in harmony
You wait till we meet, smile for me to greet

MY FARAWAY LOVE

Sun is shining, our hearts aligning
The day is so bright, I'm feeling alright
A reason to cheer, no way to feel fear
Get up to this day, just do what you say
The first morning dew, hope and dream anew
Freshness of the air, kindness must be fair
Sipping my hot tea, as I look the sea
I miss you so much, longing for your touch
One more thing to name, your love is inflame
You captured my heart, hugs and kisses start
My love is so deep, a precious to keep
Mountains between us, respect is a plus
Truly find the joy, I love you my boy
Wishing you are here, your whisper I hear
The blue sky above, hold me like a dove
Your sweet lovely voice, one of my best choice
When you are around, gently swaying sound
My night in silence, blowing of essence
Dazzling star is pure, future to ensure
No matter how far, words inside the jar
Rainbow will connect, colors to collect
Million miles away, with patience we stay
You wait till we meet, smile for me to greet

Masnavi Poetry

SHIMMERING GLITTERS

Shimmering glitters you show me a sign
Moon and stars are align
Night is indeed so bright
You have the reason to feel alright
Graceful heart that wants to care
Peaceful vibe is in the air
All best for your trip
Enjoy and make a record of sort tip
You had a loving zest
Would you put an extreme test?
Go beyond where you can reach
Make the best of it, enjoy the sweetness of peach

IF I GET THERE

Once I was in the ground
Many voices I heard around
Someone told me to get up
Walk slowly and square up
My mind wavered
My heart stuttered
I start scuffling
A bit of hope wriggling
Looking up in the stairs
I feel so scares
What will be on the top?
Should I clap and hop?
If I'll be in the center
Then it will be better
My dreams started the first step
Challenges in my footstep
With courage but still I'm barefooted
Hope and faith ferreted
If I get there, should I stay the same?
Or if I failed who to blame?
So I take a good pose
Listening and thinking my purpose
Going up is not for fame
Popularity wasn't my game

MY YELLOW FLOWER

Oh my yellow flower
My favorite one
That shine bright like a sun
You welcome my day with joy
Telling me to smile and enjoy
Oh my yellow flower
You give me more power
To start the new day
And the new beginning
Looking at you, I see hope
Like my precious love
He cares and always behind my back
To make me happy takes me aback
Oh my yellow flower
I wish to see you in the altar
While I'm walking to the aisle
Oh my yellow flower
I pray that you can hear
My wedding vow loud and clear

GULLY OF LOVE

Seven days of the week
Little pieces of my heart speak
Chirping birds on the tree tops
Opportunity that pops
A carbon that I've been waiting
Colorful vision inflating
Wondering in the skies
Monstrous dream arise
Eternal love in their eyes
Bunch of supporting advise
As I embrace the warmest hug
Droplets fall as they snug
Now I am away in the valley of love
Caring cipher of a dove
Winking in the wind
Thoughts of courage in my mind
Thousand hours without them
An inspiring and euphoric gem
The best life that I can offer
Joyous future to proffer
Their words is in my heart
My golden and essential part
The reason to let go all my fear
Million time of how they care

FAREWELL TO YOU

My heart is in the dark meadow
Broken pieces that cause pain in my airflow
All the memories that we share
Losing you which I wasn't aware
Everything will remain
Even though you are leaving and I'm in vain
If the stars answer my wish tonight
I ask for years, so you can stay in my sight
Farewell to you,
You turn the sunshine into blue
And the worst phase of waiting the dawn
Is the harsh reality of knowing you're gone
Thank you for the laughter
And your precious smile when we were together
I know this is not a goodbye for everything
Leaving behind is just the beginning
Your touched will be missed
A love for you will truly exist
It is not easy to deal with sorrow
But I know there will be sunshine tomorrow

PRICELESS MOMENT

I don't feel tired of praying
I don't feel bored of waiting
God answered what I whisper
My priceless moment of achiever
The star above shine and align
I know it must be a sign
A beautiful day and grateful occasion
Bells of life- long romantic vacation
Lovely gown and tiara on my head
My dream prince ahead
Step by step to forever
Time to cherish ever
Holding my hand and kiss
So emotional, I'm so bliss
Moment of happiness
Lifetime togetherness
As I take my wedding vow
To share joy and sorrow
A day with my destiny
A day to eternity

BLACK MAN

You are empowered
Be proud
You and me, we belong
Be strong
You are different
You've been discriminate
You've been bullied
You cry and feel ashamed
Stand!
Cheer up!
Walk with stride
Because it's your pride
You have the right to live
And enjoy life
Black, white and brown
We grow the same as human
We are all together
As one

NATURE'S CRY

Stars twinkling in this quite night
Cool wind blowing
Clear sky glowing
There is darkness but still so bright
To the flower
Sparkling power
Green forest giving out some clues
The leaves so dry
Mother Earth cry
Keep it safe and do not abuse

Amphion Poetry

MY POWER RANGER

You're an oxygen that keeps my alive
And a heart that beat for me to survive
You turn me a burning forest
Quite place you reforest
You are gravity that holding me down
Every day I want to wear a crown
You are the reason why my heart sings
I wish to have a wings
You rescue me, you're my power ranger
In this ocean of fire filled with danger
Your love is a flame that melts me
You love me so much I can see
So magical the way you caress
Your sweet voice that express
A radiance music with Joy
Life with you to enjoy
You to me are very dear
Losing you my only fear
Let our love grow and spark
I will love you everyday that's the mark

I WON'T LIE

I won't lie but I'm not alright
My world is dull and there is no light
What I am feeling inside
I have a hundred emotion to hide
The pain is getting so deep
There is a reason just to weep
Tears of crying in vain
My heart want to be free from this chain
Running to reach the shore
Dried and broken to the core
I can't scream and shout
Freezing cold inside and out
I tell myself that it's fine
Time to heal is next in line
You have stabbed my soul
Letting you go is the best role
Wounded heart full of regret
Our true story I can't forget
I'm a flower that lost all bloom
Should I deserve to be in gloom?

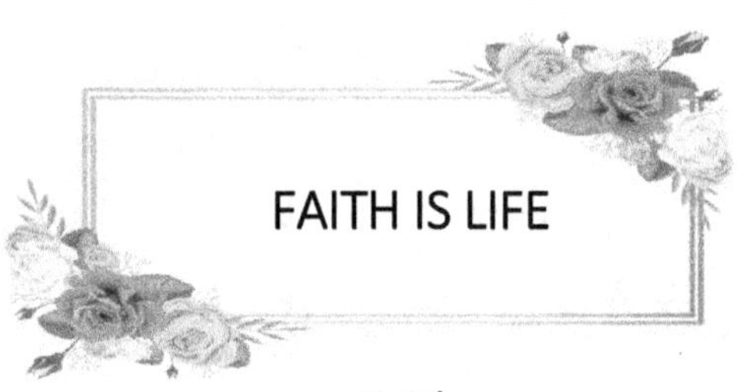

FAITH IS LIFE

Faith
In the heart
Way to reach the star
Source of hope and happiness
Stay
Stop
Wondering
How it will happen
God is there to see you through
Shine
Strong
Believing
In yourself to win
No one can move from your place
Trust
Life
A blessing
Word that has power
Trials and struggle are part
Strive

Oddquain Poetry

I DREAM OF YOU

A million stars up in the sky
You shine brightest and I can't deny
My heart beats only for you
It feels so special and so new
My morning sun smile
Beautiful diamonds by a mile
Your charismatic beauty hypnotized me
So vivid and unique to see
Walk with me under the ray of sunlight
Can you be my starlight?
In my stormy day, I want you to be my rainbow
Please give me some radiant shadow
My life is filled with glitter and sheen
Splendid and magical in between
I dream of you every single day
I don't know what to say
Life seemed to be all white and black
I need red, yellow, green and blues to pack
All of these reason and thousand more
A world with you is full of jewel decor

AUTUMN LOVE

When the sun is saying goodbye
For today, you will always be in my eyes
Like those golden leaves of autumn shine
I am still your mine.
I feel the nostalgia in the air,
Please hold me and let me feel how you care.
A final adieu from the summer memories;
Together we fly and set our boundaries.
With the wind of change and cold
I just want to feel you until we're getting old;
Let's save our promise forever
Like how mountains stay stronger.
Let's walk on leaf covered road
To restart again and decode.
The seasons may change and pass
My love for you will remain and never last.

WOMAN OF TODAY

Like that vibrant shining star

The strength to be what you are

You have all the colors of love

Radiance and shine like a dove

You are a woman, speak up and say

Don't think of challenges in your way

You have the confidence to face the world

Show your power to change in just a word

Boost to strive and do something that makes you

proud

Make yourself famous and stand out from the

crowd

Converse Poetry

OH, GOD!

Oh, God! You always make my day charming
Storm of life passes by without harming
In my battle, you give the best arming
You take control and guide me to the stall
Your sweet voice lead me the way to stand tall
You will never let me go through it all
You and me walking in the darkest trail
Protecting me always, enclose with rail
My strength is your power when I am ail
I know you have something better in store
Little smile, birds that sing, beautiful tore
I thank God for being my greatest ore

Diminishing Verse Poetry

SILENCE OF THE NIGHT

The peaceful is the silence of the night
So feel and embrace the darkness my dear
Dazzling and sparkling stars full of light
So quietly the wind is blowing slight
You sleep well and dream without tint of fear
How peaceful is the silence of the night
The blanket will take away all your fright
You look forward to have your say and clear
Dazzling and sparkling stars full of light
Smile for the golden ray will be so bright
Relax, let all your worries disappear
How peaceful is the silence of the night
Say a silent prayer, it will be all right
A new dawn to think for the perfect gear
Dazzling and sparkling stars full of light
Smile for the golden ray will be so bright
Say a silent prayer it will be all right
How peaceful is the silence of the night
Dazzling and sparkling stars full of light

Villanelle poetry

KINDNESS

Kindness is an important part
A joy to share that melts your heart
Smile to start for life to show
Don't be kind only for the sake
Real memories that you will make
Remake go ahead and know
The peace that you can never find
Empathy skills to keep in mind
Friendship bind the role you play
To strangers that don't you wish well
Your deed of goodness that will tell
A Love spell for all to say
It is a thing for happiness
And perfect pill to emptiness
Next to holiness as guide
It reflects in that loving grace
Be yourself and be in your space
Sweet act to face and replied
All things you do will be all right
Being kind will serve as your light
To heal dark night into glee
Be kind in life to teach a lot
Must present in every thought
Real knot to change and foresee

POURING RAIN

Daily water that give us strength to survive
To face today and tomorrow's strive
Golden and silver to make us smile
Hard work to dig for mile
In a world with different color
We live to success and shine with multicolor
Poverty and freedom to chase
Other people dance with sparkling lace
From fruitful harvest or in situation to worsen
Pouring rain that change the life of a person
Wide stream that can create power
Human can sealed river and destroy the highest
tower
Glamour's living in abundant land
Some are dying in an empty hand
Dazzling lights of nation was build
But when sunrise come humanity to rebuild

I CAN STAND TODAY

Through the depths of poverty

I have known want and anxiety

Going through trouble

I have known despair and struggle

I won't permit myself to think about tomorrow

No tears to shed over past and gone sorrow

As I look back upon my life

I lived no envy

I see it as a battlefield

With wrecks of dead dreams

Shattered illusions and broken hopes

Which has left me scarred and bruised

Yet I have no pity for myself

I don't forget the hardships

I learned to live each day

I can stand today

ILLUSION OF LOVE

As I had trusted you with everything
I don't know what true love is
The word love is in life
I can't describe what it is
Heartbreak is a reason of sadness
I won't believe that love exist
Our story and my heart was pure
I do not believe in love anymore
The shadows of doubt that beat
It was not my way to think
Holding on to being strong
Nothing left to nurture the soul
Love that gave me new meaning
You never felt for me
To me you truly belong
It's just an illusion
Love has a very deep meaning
You don't know what it is
I was designed to be alone
Whether I wanted it or not
You hurt me so many times
I can't still be mad

RUMOR WEEDS

Buzz buzz bees on the hilltop
The rumor weeds wink and stop
With vines tangled and open ears
A little story appears
Buzz buzz bees don't believe on what you hear
Drib drib on my cheeks
Buzz buzz bees speaks
The rumor weeds lip has wing
Waiting for someone to sing
Buzz buzz bees don't believe on what you hear
From the flowers that bloom
To the spider in loom
The rumor weeds repeat it again
How the queen bee cheat in plain
Buzz buzz bees don't believe on what you hear
Buzz buzz bees you need to be aware
The rumor weeds spread news in the air
It maybe true or not
That the rumor weeds mouth need to knot
Buzz buzz bees don't believe on what you hear

THINK IT OVER

The rainbow show up
And shadow runs after me
I try to hide
I try to walk slowly
My intention is not to leave her
But just to have a minute of peace
My mind was drained
And words was gone
I feel empty
I feel nothing
I heard myself saying to stop
Loot at the cotton cloud silently
I was amazed
Why they don't tell
Should I do the same
Or I must let the wind blow in reverse
Never allow the dark to cover you
A melody was so clear
Think it over
There will be light after darkness

OUR LOVE

Your love is my shining light
In my gloomy and darkest night
The magic that you make
My silent heart was awake
In the place where you will be
True love is what I see
You came into my life like a rose
Our Love is warm, tingles from eyes to toes
For years of being alone
Hold my hand, I'm your own
Our world full of red, green and golden ray
As you promise to be mine every day
You are my moon and I am your star
Words of forever to keep inside the jar
To build a strong castle for me and you
My sweet tender kiss pure like a dew
Our Love will stay till eternity
The brightest side of my destiny
I know that we were meant
Future to be with has a scent

DO IT AGAIN

Do it again
No one is in pain
Do your best shot in life
With courage you can hear fife
Seek answer for your soul
Then you will know your real role
Dark cloud is part of being
Make an effort and start geeing
Do it again
Your courage is within
Explore, discover and gain
Speak up your mind
And you will find
The solace of any kind
So do gather your will
Nothing to be fear, just chill
Do it again
Tomorrow is new day to begin
Let courage stay by your side
Changes the shape of tide
It will lead you too far
Until you reach the star

ONE DAY

Make your story so picturesque

Or paint picture of your past in brusque

Moments of sadness have flown

Express gratitude in full-blown

Never lost hope in every situation

Things will change in every direction

Start each day with a smile

One day you will reach the aisle

Your faded memories that you need to let go

Time to make your own life aglow

If things are old then will become new

Message of life indeed so huge to askew

Everyone has to play every puzzle each day

YOU CAN

When the dawn is dark
Don't let fear stay and mark
When you feel fright
Stay calm and wait for sunlight
If you feel down and your life in slope
Wait for the rainbow to bring a new hope
You are strong enough to pull the rope
Don't scattered tears, just taste every scope
Have will to run the race
A rocky road to walk with grace
Cheer up and show who you are
You can a play a sweet music from all your scar

FROM YESTERDAY

Cold breeze, loneliness is what I feel
I miss the voice and warmest embrace
The worst feeling that is hard to deal
Should I keep our moments or erase
My heart was broken and misplace
Oh! My shining star please stay with me
My knees was tired to chase
And nothing left to see
As the mirror telling me what is real
And my mind floating in the outer space
A heart in pain and waiting to heal
From yesterday and today in disgrace
You gave me wounds and painful trace
I am not able to find any glee
The shadow of past and mistakes in one place
And nothing left to see
While tears are dripping in the creel
And sufferings slowly efface
Your mask has fallen and mask of love reveal
It's time to end the game, I lost the race
In silent, a thousand pieces will replace
If the tide and wind agree
Soon, a grace of blossom in my vase
And nothing left to see
Like the moon and sun, a day to retrace
I can have a sweet honey as a bee
A goodbye to change in place
And nothing left to see

LEAD AND RISE

Lead to inspire others to dream and grow

Without position of desire to bestow

Self- confidence to stand in the tower

To speak in the absence of power

Solidarity to display openness

Good communication to build oneness

With a humble heart willing to listen

Understanding and respect that glisten

Positive thinking and creativity

With skills to create community

Strong voice that sounds for change

Not just for one but to everyone in range

A visionary for world to laid

Humanity in every action to aid

Experience and wisdom to share

Learning to rise is the best dare

THE GREAT FISHERMAN

Early morning he wakes up
Before the sun start to gaze
An old pants, jacket and faded hat
And the aroma of coffee to start
His eyes are widely open
While picking some courage
Before the roaster lead off to sing
Rain or shine, morning till evening
The cold wind touches his skin every day
A calm weather is what he wished
From the dark surrounding of moving ridge
A dream to feed a family
A loving wife, whispering a prayer
For her husband's safety
His boat knows what he aims
And clouds written what he plan
A good catch or nothing
In silence he waited
The patience he takes was above the waves
In the middle of nowhere and deep danger
He whistled and stayed
Thinking of his son and daughter's future
He never tired of pulling his net
For he knows the sea had something for him,
He kept paddling under the sun
And risk his life of battling the storm
A files of story to tell
This how the journey of a great fisherman begin

WALL IN BETWEEN

I'm walking to the station and I saw them
A man with a sword and a lady with costly gem
Everyone is weaving with broken lips
And they should vow with their own script
I saw men standing in gear
Stay away is what I hear
I wonder if they see
That I'm also human not flea
On the other side of the street
Someone asking for help to eat
But there is a wall in between
It is so sad that equality was unseen
Shame to our newly build society
Why justice is only done for publicity
And discrimination is everywhere
Voices marching for human rights is anywhere
I dream to live in a transparent space
Where I can't receive insult of race
And I hope for respect to hand in unity
So we can fight the undying poverty
I am the one of the struggling stone
I take a risk to sail in the unknown
You and me, we breathe in the same air
Let's hold together so there will be peace to
declare

I WRITE

I write because I have something to say
A word to lift you up every day
I write to show the reality of life
You can count it from one to five
I write to mountains and silky sea
For you to know what you didn't see
I write to share my thoughts
And I can write to stars and astronauts
I write the list of memories from the past
The most painful cuts and love that never last
I write to a single seed
To grow and give a portion for those who need
I write to my father and mother
To my amazing grandfather and grandmother
And to my little sister sorry for being so weird
Let your two dimple appeared
I write about a girl with her unreachable dreams
While she is alone in a silent stream
I write for her to speak out
She can cry, laugh and shout

ABOUT THE AUTHOR

CHRISTINE OBERAS AURELIO grew up in Basiao, Ivisan, Capiz Philippines.

She is a member of Migrant Writers of Hong Kong . She is a contributor of The Metaphors of Life Book Anthology and Arts of Poetry by Poetry Planet, Greener Start of 2022 January Edition, Dynamic Friends April Edition by Poetry Planet International Magazine, Pangyao Magazine Issue 3 by Pangyao Hong Kong Migrants Community, Issue 7 of The Tiger Moth Eco Journal of Singapore, Poetry for Ukraine, poetry in support for Ukraine publish by The Poet.

Likewise, she writes to be heard and give inspiration about the hues and shadows of her life.

"Find yourself and be yourself and be the best of whatever you are "

* 9 7 8 6 2 1 4 7 0 3 5 8 6 *